The
Backwaters
Press

An
Otherwise
Healthy
Woman

Amy Haddad

The Backwaters Press   An imprint of the University of Nebraska Press

Acknowledgments for the use of copyrighted
material appear on pages 75–76, which constitute
an extension of the copyright page.

Library of Congress Cataloging-in-Publication Data
Names: Haddad, Amy Marie, author.
Title: An otherwise healthy woman / Amy Haddad.
Description: Lincoln: The Backwater Press, an imprint
of the University of Nebraska Press, [2022] | Series:
The Backwaters prize in poetry honorable mention
Identifiers: LCCN 2021040674
ISBN 9781496227850 (paperback)
ISBN 9781496231055 (epub)
ISBN 9781496231062 (pdf)
Subjects: BISAC: POETRY /
Women Authors | LCGFT: Poetry.
Classification: LCC PS3608.A264 O86 2022 |
DDC 811/.6—dc23
LC record available at https://lccn.loc.gov/2021040674

Designed and set in Fournier MT Pro by L. Auten.

I do love nothing in the world so well as you.

—William Shakespeare, *Much Ado about Nothing*, 4.1.268–69

CONTENTS

An Otherwise Healthy Woman

In the Clutch of a Rubber Band　　　　**1**

Making Camp

The hall to intensive care is always
lit. At night, families and others,
unprepared, no gear or supplies,
make camp
in the waiting rooms, retreat
to corners, arrange makeshift
pillow forts. Lay claim to sofas,
drape and shape with sheets
to draw property lines. Downstream,
the more private consultation room
sleeps two but reeks of bad news.
The tinny heave of the coffee machine
marks time over the family burrowed
under the information desk. They stay
close in case something changes,
hover at the end of the bed ten minutes
every hour. At dawn, they bend,
stiff and rumpled at the sinks, splash
water on their faces, avoiding any
glimpses of their mirrored lives, then
pat dry with harsh paper towels.
They lean against walls
to get the best signal,
texting, talking, and casing
out who might still be there.

Cafeteria—2013

Friday night at the hospital,
way past dinner time.
The Subway counter is dark
behind its metal cage. Vending
machines, always open, hawk junk
food and sodas. What's left in
the food line is scummy water,
empty steam tables. Lemon
custard drips from the frozen
yogurt machine. The despair
of burnt coffee lingers.
A few shocked souls
in mismatched clothes
stare at turkey breast, corn and
cold fries. We point at food
we don't want. *Go eat*, we
are told. *You need to eat*,
the nurses repeat to get us out
of the unit, out of Mom's room,
out of their way.
We carry our trays
to tables in straight rows, sit
beside people we don't know,
holding our forks as if
we have never seen silverware.

Admissions

The clerk disappears behind the computer
recites all the same questions,
asked less than a week ago.
Date of birth? Name? Physician?
She answers for her husband, sits unbent
beside him. Her hair is pale sea green
permed tight at the base of her neck.
He leans forward in the unforgiving
plastic chair, head in hand
elbow on the cubicle counter. Her billfold
bulges, in the clutch of a rubber band.
She hunts one-handed for his Medicare
card, social security number, identification,
pats his knee with the other or slips her fingers
under the bar-code strip around his wrist
leftover from the last admission.
When the paperwork is done,
she helps him walk to another chair.
His room is ready, but the escort
to take him there is not.
She keeps close to him
standing vigil
alert for the wheelchair
steps away
then back again
like a mourning dove
turning in worried circles
by its dead
or dying mate.

Flexion/Extension

The hospital bed fills the small room,
forcing the dresser out in the hallway.
I sit sewing buttons on clothes I never wear,
hate mending but my hands
need to be busy, a mindless task
while I watch my Dad. The bed, a huge
metallic insect stuck on the pink hooked rugs
in my parents' room,
holds my father up so he can breathe.
I watch him out of the corner of my eye,
his chest rises erratically and falls.
He stares up at the ceiling, slowly opens then closes
his left hand, over and over.
Cupping my hand over his soft hand
that labored in music and contracts.
Dad? You okay?
He nods and as soon as I take up
my sewing, he picks up the rhythm
again, open, close, open, close.
I have seen other patients do this
sometimes, gathering up the sheet
as they do, absently not urgently,
collecting, releasing.

The Day after Memorial Day

I hug the South Lawn Road
as far as it wanders so I can find his grave.
Tiny and gray, a woman I do not know
waits next to her car while I park by the pine
that marks the family plot.
I smile briefly in her direction
as she watches me cross the road.
No salutation, she just starts
I couldn't come yesterday . . .
my husband,
she nods to the left, a field of rusty war monuments.
Unsure whether to stop
or get on with it, I walk over to her.
The clutch of white peonies I hold by my side are floppy
with dew dripping down my leg.
I am late too.
My father—I nod in the direction of the pine tree.
She leans against the car so she can
tug up her pant leg to show me.
It's these bug bites kept me from coming.
Ulcers deep and weeping,
one on her skinny ankle, another on her shin.
I stoop down to get a better look, wince
at the pain, though know she feels none.
It's okay if you're late, she says
as she lets the pant leg drop. *They understand.*

At Rehab

These are people who know their way around pulleys, braces,
     and electronic lifts. They can briskly break down a wheelchair,

flatten a walker, click open a cane with an economy of motion,
     not really looking at what they are doing.

Like raccoons washing a prized bit of food in a crystal stream,
     paws busy, efficiently working but their gaze off in the distance,

staring at the horizon or a flag being whipped by the wind
     at the other end of the parking lot.

The mother in the blue van tugs a strap to secure her limp son.
     The husband in the white car lifts his wife's useless leg in the front seat,

gently gathers her skirt round both legs. The daughter in the station wagon
     cups the crown of her father's head against the door frame then

drops the metal walker in the back. Sometimes, while loading and unloading
     the fragile cargo of their cars and vans, they catch each other's eyes,

heft the weight of each other's burdens. A mix of pity and pride settle
     in a small smile that passes briefly between them.

Then, as if nothing happened, turn their gaze back to their hands,
     close the trunk, slide the door to, and drive away.

Home Assessment

Through the eyes of a stranger,
the house looks its age with blue siding
and peeling windowsills. The therapist
counts the stairs into my mother's home,

the home where I grew up.
There is no railing by the steps.
Mom demonstrates she can walk up
without a railing. My brother and I follow

looking down, ashamed somehow
by our lack of foresight. Something about
the autumn light seems to coat each room
with a veneer of pale egg yolk. The therapist

frowns at the throw rugs, the distance from the door
to the kitchen, the height of the toilet seat.
She moves Mom's nightstand, shoves the dresser
to the opposite wall, something I would

dare not do. The therapist plops the phone
in a new spot. My mom performs tricks on command
like an ancient dog in a bad circus act, she makes
it into the tiny bathroom with her walker,

turns around slowly on her hind legs and sits
on the closed toilet. She steps, not once
but twice, in and out of the shower
using the sink and walls for balance.

At least there is a shower chair to keep us
from total failure. The therapist warns about oxygen,
clears space for a concentrator, big as a dishwasher.
We must have backup,

portable tanks in case of a power outage.
Someone must be there to crack the tanks and hook
Mom up so she can breathe. My brother and I
exchange looks of terror. The therapist moves

from room to room measuring the miles
of oxygen tubing Mom needs, tubing that trails
from her nose and drags on the floor.
Nothing else matters

to Mom but to get back home. We would agree
to any measure to make her safe
in their eyes, to get their permission
for her to return home. Something about

the light on our way out calls forth a memory
of a yellowing photograph of my brother
and me seated on the fireplace hearth in the oak-
paneled family room. I'm holding his hand.

Only two years old or so, he looks up at me,

his big sister. The clock on the mantle says 5:30.

Everything in the room is new, in its place:

the still life print overhead, carriage lamp and copper kettle,

our Mom behind the camera.

Flipping Garlic Toast

The smoke of burnt garlic, cheese, and butter fills the kitchen
as my mother rushes to the broiler to turn the bread
with her asbestos fingers.

> I move from the sink to the cutting board
> slicing tomatoes still warm from the garden.

She dodges a grandchild grabbing her legs,
crying to be picked up.

> I shout at my brother over the blare of the TV
> announcer who tallies the deaths from a tornado.

My mother recites a poem to the oven,
tosses the sizzling slices in the slender wicker
basket we use only for bread.

> "Remember me as you pass by,
> As you are now, so once was I,
> As I am now, so you must be . . ."

> I take the hot platter of steaks and sweet corn
> from my father, the smell of charcoal trailing
> behind him. He lets the screen door slap shut.

She stops, doesn't finish the rhyme,
leaves us hanging and calls everyone
to the table.

From the Motel Window

Brake lights bleed on the gray snow
as cars and buses move in and out
of the teeming parking lot. Healthy and young,
students and coaches trudge to the stadium entrance,
a swim meet, the sign says. Their words hang
in misty clouds over their heads.

She stares down from the motel window
while the tiny phone delivers crushing news.
Every detail of the scene below is burned
into her mind. She hears the words, all bad,
"tests inconclusive," "multi-system failure,"
"may not survive the night," but her attention
is on the dirty snow, the cold she cannot feel,
and the silence in the room. She pulls
the curtains behind her and leans closer
to the window looking down, trying to listen.

The grave voice on the phone
asks about next steps. She knows there are
no next steps, merely waiting for death.
She is trapped here, not where she should be.

Forever she will think this is what grief
looks like, frozen on the other side of a transparent
wall where you can see others move and breathe
but you cannot hear what they say or feel
the cold on your face and in your throat.

Whole-Berry Cranberry Sauce

I am eating the last of the whole-berry
cranberry sauce from the cans I moved
from my mother's cupboards to mine.
Cranberries were a Depression rarity
for her. I bought them almost every week
when I got her groceries. Had to crouch
to the lowest shelf in the fruit and vegetables
aisle, unless it was near the holidays
when whole cranberries held pride of place.
When she was almost blind, she would ask
for the expiration date, cock her head and print
on the lid in permanent black ink PEAS, or GB
for green beans, and then the date. The tartness
of the sauce cuts through the leftovers I eat
at my desk. I didn't even keep the lid.

The Promises Women Make to Each Other

Between mothers, daughters, and sisters
promises are extracted when frailty stops by
for a visit and does not leave. When you trip
down a few stairs, lose words, misplace keys,
all these are small reveals of what's to come.
Women start with simpler vows,
Promise you will tell me if I wear too much blush
before moving on to *Promise you will never*
put me in a nursing home.
Women know darker promises
are the hardest to speak, even
in hushed exchange: *Promise you will*
tell me if I stink, as if we lose our sense
of smell before our wits.
A promise like this exacts a bond
beyond what some can bear. Who cares
enough to whisper to you,
We need to get you cleaned up.
You are asking for intimacy more profound
than the touch of a lover.
Whom will you ask to wash
between your legs, change your clothes,
and rinse out your soiled underwear? Such pacts
keep decline and decay at bay a bit longer
while you still know the difference.

My Role as the Wife

I am the wife. My name is written on the whiteboard
    in his room between the date and the nurse's name, which changes

every twelve hours. I am a permanent member of the company.
    My most frequent line is *I am* the *wife*, not *I am his wife*.

The possessive pronoun is lost under the hospital bed with his shoes.
    My part varies little from day to day. My husband speaks off-script.

He talks about angels or other visions, except when he has a seizure.
    Either way, interrupting or convulsing, he is ignored by the rest of the cast.

I cheat and write notes on my palms. Sometimes I read right from the page.
    I memorize the lead physician's lines then repeat them to each fresh team.

We should work from the same script. Even so, the other actors have new
    pages every day that I do not see. I must improvise.

The director loves spontaneity. *Just go with it*, he whispers from the wings.
    My blocking is uninspired. Mostly, I stand by the bed where my
      husband lies.

When the call light is on, I cross left down-stage to the door, looking for help,
    waiting for a nurse to pick up the cue. My final scene is full of clichés,

empty reassurances, backward glances. I kiss his hot forehead, whisper goodbye,
    start out by drug carts and dirty linens then turn back to his room to secure

a parting promise from the night nurse, *Call me if anything changes*. I have one more
    line. *I mean it*, I say with feeling every night. The nurses nod but never call.

I am a bit player. What I say does not drive the plot. I exit to the elevator,
    barely take in the road on my drive home. The bed, like the house, is empty.

The Fit of Suffering

Go ahead. Try it on like clothes.
Pick any patient's room. So sick,
they won't even notice
when you slide the curtain
and riffle through their stuff.

Turn around to see how
suffering fits, if the sweat rings
of shock under the arms and around
the neck are your size. Pull
it on like a backpack. Gauge
the load to see what you can
bear, what brings you
to your knees.

The ER is either empty
or full of the keening kind.
Slide into the plastic chair
burning with desperation
from the last occupant.
How long can you sit still
till the heat makes you
jump to your
feet?

Try to get your breath while
wails constrict your chest and arms
before you tear suffering off
and run. The waiting rooms

are rife with it. Here you must
try it on like shoes.
Practice patience. Let one
drop then count
the minutes, the hours, the days
until the second shoe
joins its mate.

What We Did on the Floor **2**

Overture

Begin with the hands,
washing and warming first
your own.
Do not jump to lumps in the breasts.
Do not poke and prod the liver.
All other organs and body parts
will wait.
Pause, breathe, start.
Slide one index finger to the radial
pulse caught between the slender
bones of the wrist. Slow your beat
to the count you feel there. Hold
the hands as one who understands
the connection to the heart.
Treat them like the last human
hands you will ever touch.

A Guide to the Physical Exam

I. GENERAL APPEARANCE

The patient almost always brings to the examination some or, even, a
great deal of anxiety about his illness or about the examination itself.

The psych tech leans against the doorframe

of the locked unit exam room,

waiting to hand off the patient.

The October sunset slides

through the old Venetian blinds. Dust motes

float, hang in the air. The light stripes

the patient's clothes into a prisoner's

uniform. The tech leaves me alone

with him. The patient slumps on the exam

table, staring at the floor. He is still,

likely medicated on admission,

could be twenty or forty.

I close the blinds, shut the door behind me.

My first H&P with a real patient.

II. HISTORY OF PRESENT ILLNESS

The practitioner's demeanor should demonstrate self-confidence,
patience, courtesy, consideration and gentleness. All procedures
should be explained.

I tell him who I am, what I need to do,

hold out my hand. It takes a moment

before his hand takes mine. He offers

a short, mechanical shake without

eye contact. I use my calming voice:

"We will start with your history

then the physical." There is so

much to get through. I observe him.

Take him all in. I write *bland affect*

in my notes, *slowed activity,*

slow, regular breathing. He reeks

of unwashed clothes and cigarettes,

strong body odor. He smells dangerous.

I move on to questions, start the HPI,

history of the present illness.

"What brought you to the hospital?"

He whispers to his shoes,

"The cops."

III. REVIEW OF SYSTEMS

Surprise, alarm, worry, distaste or annoyance easily steal across one's
face but should be avoided.

I recall I saw him pacing the hall,

a tech by his side so he could smoke.

"They gave me a shot when I got here.

Put me in lock-up. Now I'm fucked,"

he says louder to the floor. I step

away from him. Fuss with my notes.

"My folks and the neighbors just stood there,

watched them take me away in the cruiser."

I write, *Agitated*

regarding involuntary admission.

I shift to safer ground, plow through

the review of systems, like a

litany of the saints—

Have you had fever or chills, chest pain, cough?

I pause a beat after each system

for his quiet reply, a slow motion

ping-pong. I write, *Admits to cough*

and *Denies* for everything else.

To cooperate with the examiner, the patient should be as physically
relaxed as possible. It is also important for the examiner to be relaxed.

Parents? I write, *Both alive, father*

—heart problems, mother—depressed. Smoke?

Two-pack-a-day habit.

Recreational drugs? *Admits*

to some use. Refused to say what kind.

Alcohol? *A six-pack a night.*

Not married. No children. Unemployed.

I ask him to get on the scale.

He is shaky. I place my hand

on the small of his back to balance him.

He is big, heavy but not overweight.

I take his vital signs, use the time

to steady my breath. *Vital signs all normal.*

V. ASSESSMENT

Begin your assessment of the skin with the hands, forearms and face.

I take his hands and turn them over.

Hands and arms dry and warm, nicotine-

stained fingers R hand, nails dirty

and broken. I move up to the head,

work my way down his body. He looks

past me, impassive, compliant. Scalp,

sinuses, *Nontender to palpation.*

I look in his nose, pull his ears

up then back to straighten the canals.

I tap my tuning fork on my palm,

hold it near each ear, he nods, smiles a bit.

"No one has done that to me before,"

he says. I shine a penlight in his mouth.

"Say 'Ahhh.'" He gags. *Tongue coated, yellow teeth.*

I place my hands around his neck,

feel the thyroid slide against my fingers

as he swallows. I probe the tender

hollow under the mandible,

deep in the angles formed by clavicles,

feel for lumps and realize

I forgot the eyes.

VI. EXAMINATION OF THE EYES

Visual Fields by the Confrontation Method. Position yourself so that your face is directly in front and on the level with his.

He meets my eyes with his jaundiced

ones. He covers his left,

I cover my right. I am the normal

against which he will be measured.

"Tell me when you see the pencil."

Like magic, the pencil appears

from behind his shoulder. "Now," he says,

"Now."

VII. EXAMINATION OF THE OPTIC DISC

It may sometimes be necessary to cause the patient some discomfort or pain in order to assess his condition accurately. The practitioner must be willing and able to do this too, without undue anxiety or guilt and with matter-of-fact dispatch.

I look deeper into his eyes.

My thumb on his eyebrow, I catch

the red reflex of the pupil with my scope.

My fingers brush his lips and cheek

as I enter his eye with my blinding light.

He bears my clumsy moves,

stares straight ahead at the wall

as I told him to do. *Optic discs*

bilaterally yellowish.

VIII. AUSCULTATION OF THE LUNGS AND HEART

The patient should be supine or lying with his upper body elevated to 30–
45 degrees. The room must be quiet.

Back to his chest where I left off,

I ask him to remove his shirt

and take deep breaths. I listen through his sighs

to his crackling lungs. I focus next

on the heart, position the diaphragm

over the aortic valve

and immediately hear the low

slushy lub-dub of my first real murmur.

I lean in until my hair touches

his chest, tune out everything but

the faulty beat. So intent

on the timing of this abnormality,

I forget where I am.

Blame Placing

Holding the scalpel in his gloved hand
like a baton, poised above the black crust
that was once her big toe—
tap, tap, tap, ready, begin.
The already hardened
medical students and residents
flank the maestro.
I stand by the head of the bed,
reach for the patient's hand,
hold it in both of mine.

The surgeon cuts away
at the decay
with constant clinical patter.
At first the patient does not flinch,
her hand held in mine.
She grips me, bites
her bottom lip, holds her breath
against the pain.

Now we're getting somewhere.
See how it bleeds. That's a good sign,
he instructs. I whisper in her ear,
Take a deep breath.
It will help ease the pain.
The smallest cry escapes
as she exhales. She turns crimson.

The performance interrupted,
he addresses me, *Nurse, let go of her hand.*
She grabs me tighter.

He drops the scalpel,
snaps off both sterile gloves.
I want to see you in the hall, now!
Extracting my hands,
I follow him out of the room.

He punctuates each word with a jab
to my chest, just above my name tag,
When I tell you to let go
of my patient, do it.

He pivots to leave. Not quite finished
he turns back, face so close to mine
I feel his breath, *You made things worse*
by babying her. Students in tow
who watched their mentor's show
follow.

I return to dress her bloody foot,
hope that there is something ordered
for her pain. *I'm sorry,*
I got you in trouble, she says.

Dehiscence

You have come unstitched.

Holes appear on your threadbare abdomen.
Tunnels develop and connect bowel, liver, pancreas.
Enzymes ooze out and digest your skin,
no matter how hard we try to stem the flow.
A jerry-rigged system to
hold together our mistakes.
The stench is overwhelming, ever present,
reminding everyone, but especially you,
that you have come undone.

Since the truth is too horrible to grasp,
since I can offer you nothing else,
I clean you up.
I wash your face,
brush your teeth,
comb your hair,
turn you on your side,
push soiled linens away,
roll clean sheets under you,
remove layers and layers of damp dressings,
and replace them with new dressings and tape.

I give you the certainty and calmness of my motions,
the competence and comfort of my touch
as I smooth the top sheet over my work.
Done.

For a few pristine moments, we allow ourselves
to be caught in the illusion of your wholeness.

Gallows Humor

PART I

It was late at night as we worked on our nursing care plans for OB/GYN the next morning. We were not yet twenty years old and terrified about what would be expected of us. None of us had witnessed a birth before. We wanted our care plans to be perfect.

We helped each other with terms and words that were foreign to us, looking them up in our olive-green *Taber's Cyclopedic Medical Dictionary*. Thumbing through the *M* section in my *Taber's*, I spied the word "monster." I read the definition aloud, "A grossly deformed individual, usually due to faulty development. The word should never be used when discussing such a patient with those who are emotionally attached to him or her. Terms such as handicapped, congenitally deformed, or abnormal would be more appropriate." We got the idea to replace the word "newborn" with "monster" in our care plans. The instructions for baby's first bath now read, "Fill the tub with about three inches of water that feels warm but not hot. Bring the monster to the bath area and undress her completely. Gradually slip the monster into the tub feet first, using one hand to support her neck and head."

PART II

When the crumbling psychiatric hospital, Our Lady of Victory, was remodeled, the administration encouraged the staff to brainstorm new names for the hospital to match the new look; a ploy to distract us from caring for psychotic patients among the demolition dust and danger. We were told to think of a name that didn't sound like winning a war but something that would look welcoming over the entrance and make patients want to be admitted. The brainstorming session quickly degraded when someone shouted, "Spring Inn," the name of a neighborhood bar near the hospital. We found names of other bars in town like Dew Drop Inn, The Recovery Room, and The Last Resort. Then we made up names: Dementia Den, The Padded Cell, The Poop Deck, Cuckoo Cove, and Psycho Susie's. For a week or so, we thought this was hysterical. When they named it "The Center for Mental Health," we stopped playing the game.

Second-Degree Block

For more than three decades, I have saved
the fine etching of your dying
in a recipe box where I kept 3 × 5 cards
on which I painstakingly printed
words like *antiarrythmic* and *cardiotonic*.
I used the cards to tell my instructor
about the drugs I would give
and why, even though
I didn't really know.

The EKG strips are pale green graph ribbons
clipped to the drug card for digoxin
to "slow and strengthen the heart."
I have underlined these words.
The problem was with conduction,
not the muscle, I see now.
The electrical circuits of your heart were faulty,
like old, stripped wires,
the message haphazardly getting through to the ventricles
as the spaces between the spidery spikes grew wider.

As we stared at the bank of monitors in the nurses' station,
I only had eyes for the one labeled "Room 4."
When your heart misfired, I froze the screen
and hit the print button.
I learned to measure the length of your failure
with a ruler, to place tiny precise marks
between the QRS peaks and valleys
and the roll of the t wave.
Dutifully, I counted the miniscule squares,

noted the times on the back of the strips,
each hour the rhythm a little worse.
I took them home to practice measuring,
never tracing them back to you.

The White Stucco House

Even after forty years, the house makes me shudder
when I drive by. I visited that house. Twice.
A depressed housewife and her husband

lived there then. I slow my car to see what remains.
The yard now holds a tree swing and a blue plastic pool,
the detritus of children.

I made home visits to see the wife after her discharge.
She was my one-to-one patient.
We agreed to meet once a week to talk,

keep her on her meds, keep her out of the hospital.
That was my plan. The first time I knocked on her door,
she was home alone. She settled me

in the white and gold living room.
From the kitchen, a coffee percolator moaned like a tiny ghost.
She carried china cups on a metal tray that rattled.

The plate of cookies almost fell to the floor.
She shook as she poured coffee into cups
thin and pale like her. I asked questions.

All her answers were single words.
I was blind to her eyes flicking to the clock and windows.
Deaf to the fear humming in the walls.

Next visit, the husband was home.

Without a word, he looked me up and down,

then walked into the kitchen.

When the wife and I started to talk, the racket began,

softly at first. He swore under his breath,

the tirade at a low boil. Explosive curses punched the air.

All bluff and sputtering, he seemed to me a cartoon.

The storm grew with a crash of pans flung

into the sink, the cupboard doors slammed shut and shut.

She jumped with each salvo.

I clung to my mental health questions, clueless

to the menace. She didn't answer me, so I cut my visit short.

At the door, she asked me not to come again

and softly clicked the door shut. That was my last visit.

I didn't tell anyone why.

Let me make it clear. I left her there alone with him.

Families Like This

Speak too loudly, stink from sweat
and beer. Thrown together
like strings of Christmas lights
jammed in a bin
where some work and some don't.
Jessamyn's mine, the mother explains.
Lonnie's ours.

Families like this carry pocket
knives in their overalls. Use one
to cut their boy down from the swing set,
where he hung in the rain.
Lay his body on the slide,
wait for the squad. *It was raining*

that day or we wouldn't never
had looked out the window, never
would've found him at all. It was
raining. They repeat the story
to the flock in the waiting room.

Families like this are wary

and
watchful, agree
to every test and treatment.
Never ask the health team
questions, only nod.
Families like

this worship before
the heart monitor, spy miracles

in each muscle twitch or sigh
from the
ventilator. But, this family
doesn't believe in our religion.
This family watches their son,
turns their backs to the heart
rate skimming across the
screen, not taken in by this
false god.

After only two days in the ICU,
the mother tells the team
he is gone.
Stolid, clear-eyed,
this family has
drawn a line. Too soon for us,
the team fights for him. He is so young.
We shift to high code to murmur about
their survivor guilt, premature closure.

The family circles the bed.
His stringy black hair stark
against the pillow, his teenage
whiskers dust. They
wait
for the team to get it. Willing

us to stop. Not what we expect
from families like this.

The Course of Leukemia

Between searching the luncheon specials, catching up and small talk, she offers a précis of agony. Her whispered chronicle of loss holds me while the waiter moves clockwise around the table taking orders. Behind our menus, she recounts a shorthand version of her husband's dying as the rest of the party struggles with hard choices about soup or salad. The clink of silver and splash of water and ice drift around us, muffling her words: "He had fevers over 104 degrees, chills. I had to pick him up from the floor so many times. He was a big man. You remember, right? Bled. Such a mess. I'd ask him, 'Are you in pain?' 'No,' he'd say. Always, 'No.' Horrible. So thin. Just horrible. Bruised so easily. So hard for me, for him at the end." Only the briefest pause. "Oh. Just a second. Let me see. I think I'll have the duck, thank you, and water's okay. With lemon, please." I am next, trying to focus on an entrée.

Day's End at the Farmer's Market in Montparnasse

Wooden crates in crisscrossed stacks
on the slate-gray sidewalk spill fuchsia
tissue papers that once cupped Anjou pears.
Pale-gold, cracked Cavaillon melons
spit seeds among discarded mâche
and stray strawberries marking
the borders of the now vacant, makeshift stalls.

Just ahead of the brutal steel brushes
of the street cleaner, an old woman
in a lipstick-red hat draws
a linen handkerchief from her purse,
flicks it open as if waving to someone,
bends down and rescues a perfect white peach.

Ten Items or Less

I can spot them
even in the checkout line.
Putting the rubber stick
between their oranges and my bread,
their hands are
marked with purple, green,
and yellow bruises.
I know where they have been,
the needle sticks just the start of it.

The bruise tattoos,
each prick leaving its history.
I match the hand to the face,
looking for signs of what is killing them
as they sort coupons
for cereal or canned tomatoes.

Cut along the Lines   **3**

Stereotactic Biopsy

Climb up here.
The table is so high there are stairs.
Lie down with your breast through the hole.
The table is very hard.
I surrender my right breast,
the tech pulls on it.
She raises the table even higher.

Face down, turned to the wall,
arms straight by my side.
The bright light from a desk
traces my silhouette black against the white wall.
I can see the outline of my head, shoulders,
the dip of my back.

She tugs and adjusts.
The site is close to your armpit.
We need as much breast tissue through the hole as possible.
My breast does not cooperate.
After many X-rays, sighs of frustration,
the position is right.

I cannot move.
Do not move.
Her voice from somewhere below me.
A swish of air, the doctor enters.
No preliminaries to the tech or me.
Without warning,
a sharp burning in my breast.
I gasp.

This will numb the site.
Now this will be loud,
sort of a bang.
It won't hurt.
Don't flinch, the tech warns.

Each time,
sixteen times,
she puts her hand on the small of my back,
a warning touch
just before the gunshot sound.
The wide-bore needle pierces my breast,
taking a tunnel of tissue.

Okay, the doctor says,
Let's see what we've got.
A rustle of footsteps, the door opens and closes.
The room is absolutely still.
I stare at my outline on the wall.
Trapped.
Waiting.
Where did they go?

Thinking I am alone,
I start to cry quietly
then sob.
Between my first great gasping breath
and the next,
the doctor clears his throat.

Nuclear Bone Scan

I am cocooned in the tube, held in the light. I am
translucent on the blue screen. The long thigh bones
are hollow, the pelvis a shallow bowl that cradles
the coccyx, tail of the spine. My feet are trussed together
with a thick rubber band. Arms bound at my sides,
I recite a Rosary, barely touching thumb to each finger
to count the decades, recalling only one set of Mysteries—
Joyful. It takes an hour for my body to inch forward
out of the tube. The top of my head escapes first,
then my eyes, blinded by the overhead light
covered with a plastic photo of cherry blossoms
and azure sky that I might see lying under a tree.
I stare at the image and count the leaves
as the rest of my body emerges. Before sliding me back
in the tube once more, the tech explains they will now
scan the skull. A grimace and deep-set empty holes
take shape. I steal glimpses at the screen above the tube
to the left. The ghost of a half-foot skeleton just traceable
with smoky edges materializes. I search for the glow
that signals the invasion has spread to my bones.
The isotope dots fill in the spine, sacrum, true and false
ribs, the axial and appendicular. I shift only my eyes.

I cannot move my head. Guilty, as if peeking at
pornography, I never get to see the final impression
of my finely wrought frame. The radiologist keeps the
pictures to himself and releases only words.

An Otherwise Healthy Woman

Has crushing chest pain
Faints during choir practice

Feels a lump in her breast
Loses her way home

Is incontinent on the bus
Forgets her daughter's name

Finds despair cloaked by underwear
Shoulders the burden

Bruises too easily
Cries when she means to laugh

Passes it off as nothing
Waits for the next betrayal.

Infidelity

Old friends I haven't seen
in a while don't recognize me
with short hair. I tell them all
the same thing—easy,
wash and go, so cool
in the summer. I don't tell them
my hair left me, like an adulterous
spouse, didn't even pack
a bag, just blew out the door.
Left a few strands lonesome
as a single sock at the back of a drawer.
Oh, there were signs,
warnings from women who got
the same treatment.
Perhaps for others, I thought. My hair
and I would never part.
Months later, desperate and scared,
I welcomed the first wisps back, clung
to every strand though the color
and feel were different, coarse and gray.
I am still watchful,
asking each hair caught in the drain,
Where do you think you're going?

Chemotherapy Lounge

"I don't understand this, I only turned my back for a few seconds.
All our money was in there."

"Up next: Daydreaming about sex and why it's good for you."

The televisions talk for us,
fill the endless spaces.
There is no understanding.
Tacit treatment of cancer patients
who are all alike.
Lined up in lounge chairs,
at times almost fifty of us.

"Welcome back. We're talking about how to have house guests and enjoy them."

"What makes your adrenaline rush? What makes it pump?"

The faintly metallic odor of noxious drugs,
the sour-sweet overlay of vomit
permeates everything, even the carpet.
Trapped in our seats,
plugged to poles,
we sit for hours.
Poisoning takes time.

"It was to be a yearly lease but I let him have it month to month.
Then he wanted me to pay for the utilities.
I said, 'Do you want me to fix your breakfast, too?'"

"Let's get together for dinner and finalize the details about the wedding."
"Sorry, Roxanne, not tonight."
"But darling, why?"

The nurse has on a felt pumpkin hat.
She sits heavily on a stool by my side,
drops ten or so filled syringes in her lap.
All of this will go into my body.
"So, how've you been?"
she asks without looking at me.

I feign sleep, try to shut out
noise and small talk.
Neither one of us is really here.
Magenta Adriamycin crawls
up the tubing to the port
just above my bra.

*"Tanya, welcome to our show. Tell us why things haven't been going so well
between you and Roger."*

*"Storms will fire up north, expect some wind damage,
it'll juice up down south with heavy rain."*

The taste of the drug
hits me as soon
as it slips past the port.
My tongue itches.
I whisper,
"I'm so sick."
A reflex pat on the arm,
emesis basin and towel in reply.

"Now your clothes can smell like you just hung them out to dry in the sunshine."

"When are you going to tell him the baby isn't his?"

What I need
is a large breasted woman—
pale-yellow house dress,
worn, blue-plaid apron.

I catch the scent of Vel soap
as she enfolds me on her old porch glider.
Bridal wreath in full bloom
shades us as we rock back and forth

She rubs my back
with a depth of compassion I can collapse in
and never bottom out
while she softly repeats,
"What a terrible thing to happen to you, honey.
What a terrible thing."

Post-Op

The hidden losses are legion.
The subtle, sensual brush of fingers
pushing back my hair, face slightly tilted,
eyes half-closed
the signal of seduction or innocent flirting—
all gone. Cut off.
Presentable, neat, clean but
not spontaneous
no unconscious sense of self as beautiful.
My dearest love replaces uncontrolled
passion with pity
lust with measured gentleness.
The rush that sped from nipple to groin
now numb
and sidetracked to my mind
remembering in the loss,
the cost
of survival.
In dreams
past lovers begin a caress
fingers brushing down my neck
and even in deepest sleep
I stop their hands.

Cat Scan

Inches from my nose, she inspects me
through slivered parakeet-green eyes
scanning through soft tissue, muscle, bone
on a level no CT or MRI can reach.
My black and orange calico
places her clawless paws
on the red crescent scar
where my breast used to be.
Inner lids slowly veiling her eyes
she kneads my chest
paws opening and closing
purring in rhythm
head down.
I trace a single line
from the bridge of her nose
up to her ear
ending under her chin.

Chemotherapy Side Effects

A wave swells higher,
smells, even the thought of food,
push sour bile up.

A well black and deep,
straight slippery walls that
seep the will to escape.

A prick of claws at the throat,
something runs down
the spine, the heart stops.

A rill, then river.

Pried from milkweed pods,
hair like floss floats
seedless.

A stone set below the breastbone.

French Weaving for Damages

Invisible mending, this technique is done on select
fabrics with small tears, holes, and burns.

Surgeons have sewn me back together,
not all at once, but over time

with individual thread strands from hidden
areas, such as inseams or cuffs,

or resected muscle and skin
reattached from back to chest,

woven into the damaged area by hand.
How ever expert the stitches

there are spots inside me that still gape.
Tears only I can fix.

Some fabrics don't always lend
to completely invisible results.

For those I need illusion net
to bridge the space, placing the right size

square, careful to match the original structure.
I pick up threads of who I was,

creating new fabric as it closes the whole
hiding the deeper damage.

The untrained eye cannot detect the repair.
To feel the flaws that remain,

the ongoing healing within,
run your fingers over my skin.

Before- and After-Breasts

In a place where every woman who waits is in pain
the chairs are wooden and hard. The plastic

surgeons hire only beautiful receptionists who
wear pink smocks to show off their tasteful

cleavage. I await dismemberment
and reconstruction. No choice about losing

my breasts. Some choice about what I could
do to hide my loss, too weak or proud

for a flat chest and the judgment of strangers.
I pass the time before my appointment

with a photo album placed in my lap by a young
woman in pink who gets to keep her breasts.

I have seen this kind of book in pricey salons,
a portfolio of the master's work,

of lovely models with exquisite haircuts.
This book is filled with headless women,

hands on hips, cut off at the navel
paired up as before and after

photos of breasts, pages of breasts.
The before-breasts droop in the way

breasts do that have been used for
food and lovemaking, breasts that give

to the pull of time. The after-breasts look
startled, at attention, and always bigger

than the before-breasts. *Think of this
as an opportunity to have*

the breasts you've always wanted,
the plastic surgeon pitches to me.

A used-car salesman, he examines
my trade-ins, their wear and tear,

mismatched size and memories.

Port-a-Cath

Button made of skin,
easy access to my veins.
Easy as a whore,
blank-eyed and indifferent,
opening to the syringe.

When chemo is through,
I ask to have it removed.
The silver scar stays
peeking out above my bra,
shining at dinner parties.

Dark Rides

Fat, dumb and happy, assured I was

        cured; unaware for years

I was waiting in line, inching forward,

        pushed past the sign

You must have this much cancer

        to ride. Ka-thunk.

An empty car arrives. I'm next.

        I hurl through swinging doors

into darkness. I hear the muffled gasps

        and moans of other riders.

Death pops up out of nowhere, skeletons sit next to me

        in waiting rooms in this living nightmare.

The illusion of collision is ever present,

        even with my eyes closed. Other rides

provide a warning of the doom ahead:

        keep your hands and arms inside the car,

grasp the bar at the front of your seat.

        Pay attention to what normal feels like.

Get ready to lose it

        in a stomach-dropping moment. My dark

ride has no rules. It just

      blindly jerks forward with no connection

between the stunts until the doors crash open

      piercing me with light.

High-Wire Act

The catch phrases in the drug ads catch
nothing
of the reality. The diagnosis is a tightrope.
I am the walker doomed to tread
with a balance pole teetering between
hope and despair. I walk for three
or four months, legs bent, concentrating,
tipping slightly left or right,
until the wire is cut
sending me freefalling into the certain doom
of recurrence, or if the scans are clear,
a brief respite
before I start the next act of derring-do
on the high wire.

New to the Joint

We old hands curl back in our recliners

> like crabs tucked into

> a vacant shell.

Our bodies are here but our minds

> float fuzzy with sedatives

> and chemo.

The air changes, fills with the scent of soap

> and vanilla. Someone new takes the

> empty chair in our corner.

We watch the novice drop purse and phone

> by her seat. The beads on her wrist

> clatter when they start her iv. She asks

What do you have? She breaks Rule One:

> never ask what you're in for. Yet,

> *Breast, breast, lung,*

we say in rhythmic order. Emboldened,

> she shatters Rule Two, tells us her

> secret crime,

I have a big old tumor around my aorta,

          her voice full of shy hope. We try

          to control

the soft whines in our throats we dare not

          share for we are beaten dogs. We

          know she is on death row.

If our chairs were not made of lead,

          we would push back from her

          flimsy hold

on life. We will not steal

          her innocence. We fold

          into ourselves far away.

Ode to a Freckle above My Left Breast

Resigned to losing all that was mine
I brace myself before the bathroom mirror
in the hospital room. Afraid to look
at the wreckage where
my breast had been, what joy to see
you survived the assault! You perch above
the carnage where you always sat.
Spared from the surgeon's knife
you are a tiny flag of resistance
claiming territory, protecting a small part
of my chest from razing and reconstruction.
I press my palm over you, feel the heat rise
off my wounds. When the surgeon rounds,
I thrust a bouquet of lavender roses
from the overbed table into her arms,
the only thanks-offering I have for you.

Oarsmen at Chatou

How many times have I stood like this?
Grabbing the cold bar overhead,
white-knuckled as if I must hold myself up.
The tech arranges my chest and chin,
presses my back closer to the flat, metal plate.
Don't move. Take a deep breath. Hold it.
I stare at the painting on the wall
not three feet from my nose.
In a slender gig, an oarsman in straw boater, red
sash beckoning to the empty seat.
A lady and gentleman pose undecided
among the rushes and cattails at water's edge.
An assistant straddles the bow ready to push off.
Okay. Let it out. Stay put while I check the film.
Her orange jacket nips at the waist, velvet
I decide, lace cuffs. She lifts her long blue skirt
to save it from the mud. A spotless petticoat,
bright as the light on the river, shines below.
The first few years, I saw neither boat nor river,
only smudges of blue and white, a golden streak.
A few more years, the figures took shape.
I understand now why her head is turned
away from the boat. She doesn't want to die.

Cut along the Lines

After hours of signing consents, I am finally ready

       to go under the knife. A sedative blurs

the world. I drift away, but someone pulls

       me upright, unties my gown, lets it fall

to my waist. I feel a marker drawing on my bare chest.

       I hear it squeak across my skin. I see a bold

"YES" on my left breast. Groggy, weak, limp,

       I reason, *Oh, they want to make sure*

they cut off the right one. The drawing trails under

       my left arm, charting how to divide me,

where to dissect my latissimus dorsi

       from its origin in my back to cobble a breast.

The surgeon draws letters, arrows, and dashes, a cut diagram

       like those made for butchering steers. *Chuck*

dash—dash—dash, sits next to Ribs, dash—dash—dash

       above Brisket. They mark the primal cut

to save precious muscle. No one warned me

       this would happen—the drawing. No one told

me my body would be used as a whiteboard of reminders

       for the surgeon. They don't have to tell me these minor

details. I will not die from the mark-up, but I retain

       the permanence of the black ink.

Jug Shots

Turn to the left
put your hands on top of your head. Hold it.
Okay, now face forward
hands on your hips.
Stripped to the waist in front of a blue screen,
in the surgeon's exam room, my stretched and distorted
chest is the object of the camera.
The implants sit on my ribs under my muscles,
part of me now, yet cool and alien. The blonde
perky tech clicks shots cutting me off at the neck.

Okay, one more close-up.
Too late, my hand flies up to cover
my aquamarine necklace. Flushed
and embarrassed, I don't want this part of me
in the pictures. She starts over:

Do you want to try a tattoo areola and nipple?
They wash off. We're letting patients test them.
Numb, I let her paste the photos on the blank
mounds where my breasts used to be.
The tattoos burn through my blouse
as I leave the office, smoldering
nipples constantly erect.

Later in the shower, I watch someone else's nipples
dissolve and drip down my stomach and legs into the drain.

Bottom of the Cup

The shop still serves tea but I am here for the psychics
to peer into my future, a place no one I know will see me go
a few blocks off Jackson Square. I ask for the whole deal:
a private booth, like a confessional, tarot and palm
readings, and an audio recording to replay later.
I pull aside the velvet curtain, limp with heat and humidity,
sit, listen to the snap of cards and murmurs
through the thin walls on either side. My diviner appears
in an orange silk shirt, ratty at the cuffs, with the kindest eyes
that ever held mine. Lined and weatherworn,
a slight tremor in his hands, he says he quit
teaching long ago, has the gift like his mother. Best
to use it. After setting up the recorder,
he clears his throat and asks, *Chère, what do you want to know?*
I planned to say nothing of my hopes and fears
to test what he could see, but something breaks in me.
He traces the lines of my life and tells me:
There are menacing clouds in your future. This I know is true.
These dark times will pass so don't worry, Chère.
I see a long life and love. I don't believe him,
but he repeats it even so,
I see love.

The Commercial Version of Metastatic Breast Cancer

My only model for how to live

my life after the diagnosis is the woman

in the TV ad who rises at dawn, slips out of bed

in yoga clothes, pats her golden retriever,

kisses her handsome graying husband,

makes coffee, steps outside for the paper,

gazes at the clouds in prayerful repose.

She is living the new normal.

If these images do not fit, the drug company

tailors another life for me to try on.

I must fashion myself as the owner

of a knitting shop on Main Street USA,

and although I do not knit, here I teach classes,

help people pick out yarn and needles.

My husband brings me lunch. We eat

and smile at each other, thankful for the sandwich,

dog, yoga clothes, coffee, sunrise, clouds, yarn.

At night, we picnic with friends,

or is this my pregnant daughter and her husband?

We all look at the sonogram, smile some more.

We blow bubbles with our grandchildren, or is that

another drug company ad? Some things

have changed, the voiceover intones. Act

normal and no one will notice.

ACKNOWLEDGMENTS

I wish to thank the editors of the following journals and books, in which these poems, sometimes in earlier versions, first appeared:

Annals of Internal Medicine: "Families Like This"

The Arduous Touch: Women's Voices in Health Care, ed. Amy Haddad and Kate Brown (West Lafayette IN: Purdue University Press, 1999): "Blame Placing"

Bellevue Literary Review: "The Day after Memorial Day"

Between the Heartbeats: Poetry and Prose by Nurses, ed. Cortney Davis and Judy Schaefer (Iowa City: University of Iowa Press, 1995): "Dehiscence"

Fetishes: "Post-Op"

The Healing Muse: A Journal of Literary and Visual Arts: "From the Motel Window"

Health Humanities Reader, ed. Therese Jones, Delese Wear, and Lester D. Friedman (New Brunswick NJ: Rutgers University Press, 2014): "Second-Degree Block"

Intensive Care: More Poetry and Prose by Nurses, ed. Cortney Davis and Judy Schaefer (Iowa City: University of Iowa Press, 2003): "Port-a-Cath," "Ten Items or Less"

Janus Head: "Jug Shots"

The Journal of General Internal Medicine: "Chemotherapy Lounge"

The Journal of Medical Humanities: "Cat Scan," "Flexion/Extension"

Reflections on Nursing Leadership: "At Rehab"

Stories of Illness and Healing: Women Write Their Bodies, ed. Marsha Hurst and Sayantani DasGupta (Kent OH: Kent State University Press, 2007): "Stereotactic Biopsy"

24/7/365: The International Journal of Healthcare and Humanities: "The Course of Leukemia"

The title for part 2, "What We Did on the Floor," is taken from Marie Howe's "Practicing," in *What the Living Do* (New York: Norton, 1998). The epigraphs for each section of "A Guide to the Physical Exam" are from Barbara Bates, *A Guide to Physical Examination* (Philadelphia: J. B. Lippincott, 1974).

My special gratitude to the faculty in the MFA program at Queens University in Charlotte, North Carolina. Thanks to fellow poets who provide support and feedback, especially Fred Pond, Courtney LeBlanc, Caroline Earleywine, Ashley Steineger, Chelsea Risley, and Barbara Costas Biggs. A special thank you to Sue Burkhard, who kept me organized every step of the way.

BACKWATERS PRIZE IN POETRY

2020 Nathaniel Perry, *Long Rules: An Essay in Verse*
     Honorable Mention: Amy Haddad, *An Otherwise Healthy Woman*

2019 Jennifer K. Sweeney, *Foxlogic, Fireweed*
     Honorable Mention: Indigo Moor, *Everybody's Jonesin' for Something*

2018 John Sibley Williams, *Skin Memory*

2017 Benjamín Naka-Hasebe Kingsley, *Not Your Mama's Melting Pot*

2016 Mary Jo Thompson, *Stunt Heart*

2015 Kim Garcia, *DRONE*

2014 Katharine Whitcomb, *The Daughter's Almanac*

2013 Zeina Hashem Beck, *To Live in Autumn*

2012 Susan Elbe, *The Map of What Happened*

2004 Aaron Anstett, *No Accident*

2003 Michelle Gillett, *Blinding the Goldfinches*

2002 Ginny MacKenzie, *Skipstone*

2001 Susan Firer, *The Laugh We Make When We Fall*

2000 David Staudt, *The Gifts and the Thefts*

1999 Sally Allen McNall, *Rescue*

1998 Kevin Griffith, *Paradise Refunded*

The Backwaters Prize in Poetry was suspended from 2005 to 2011.

To order or obtain more information on these or other University of Nebraska Press titles, visit nebraskapress.unl.edu.

Printed in the USA
CPSIA information can be obtained
at www.ICGtesting.com
CBHW032235080324
5160CB00003B/313